O HOLY NIGHT
Christmas Classics for Solo Piano

by Alex-Zsolt

Moderately Advanced

PUBLISHING COMPANY

lillenas.com

Contents

O Holy Night

with

Silent Night! Holy Night!

ADOLPHE C. ADAI
Arr. by Alex-Zsc

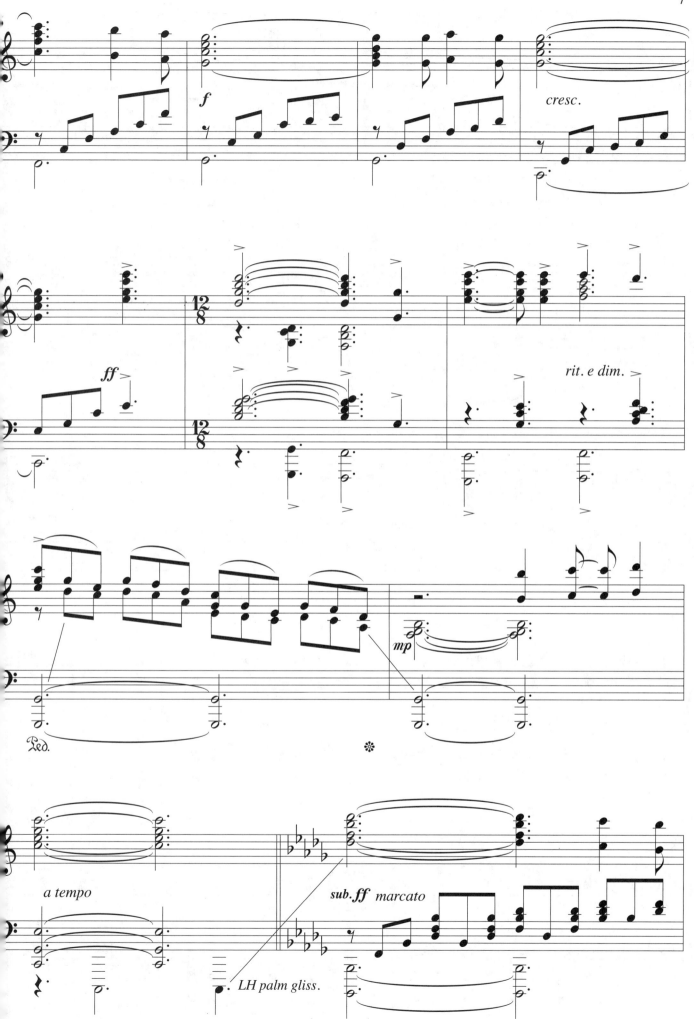

Adagietto ♩ = ca. 80   *"Silent Night! Holy Night!"

accel.

a tempo
mf *dolce*

cresc.   ten.   *mp*

ten.

music by FRANZ GRUBER.

Sing We Now of Christmas

Lively ♩ = ca. 70

French Carol
Arr. by Alex-Zsolt

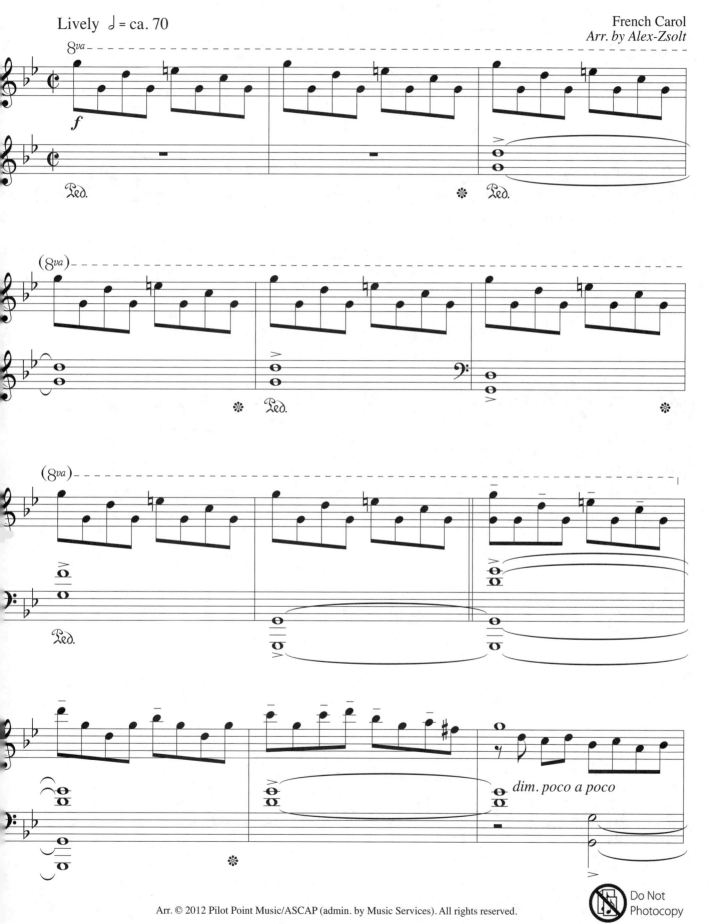

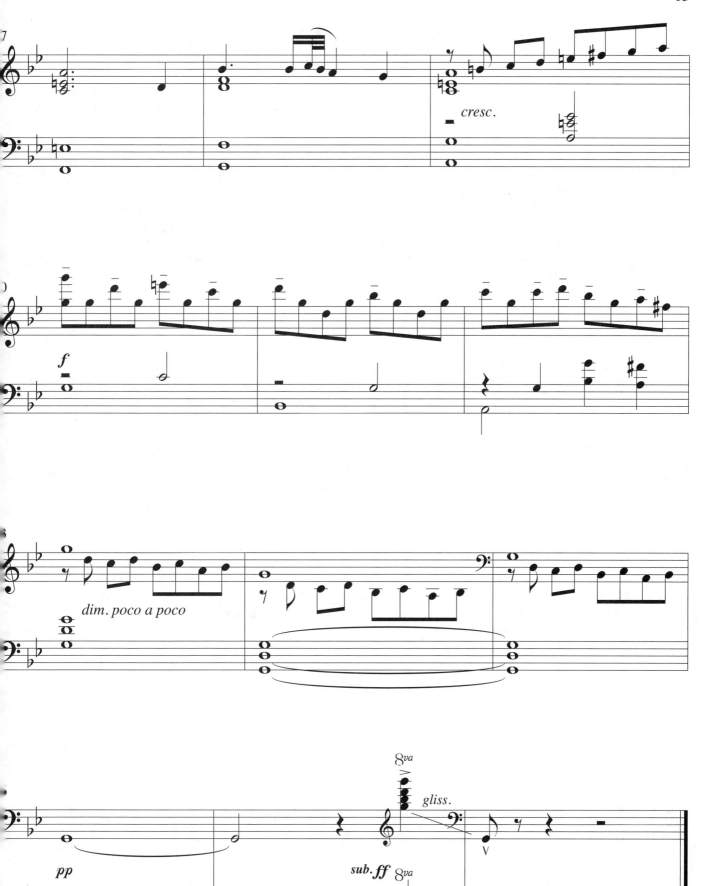

Away in a Manger

JAMES R. MURRAY an
WILLIAM J. KIRKPATRIC
Arr. by Alex-Zso

Angels We Have Heard on High

with

Hark! the Herald Angels Sing

Angels, from the Realms of Glory

Traditional French Melod

Arr. by Alex-Zso

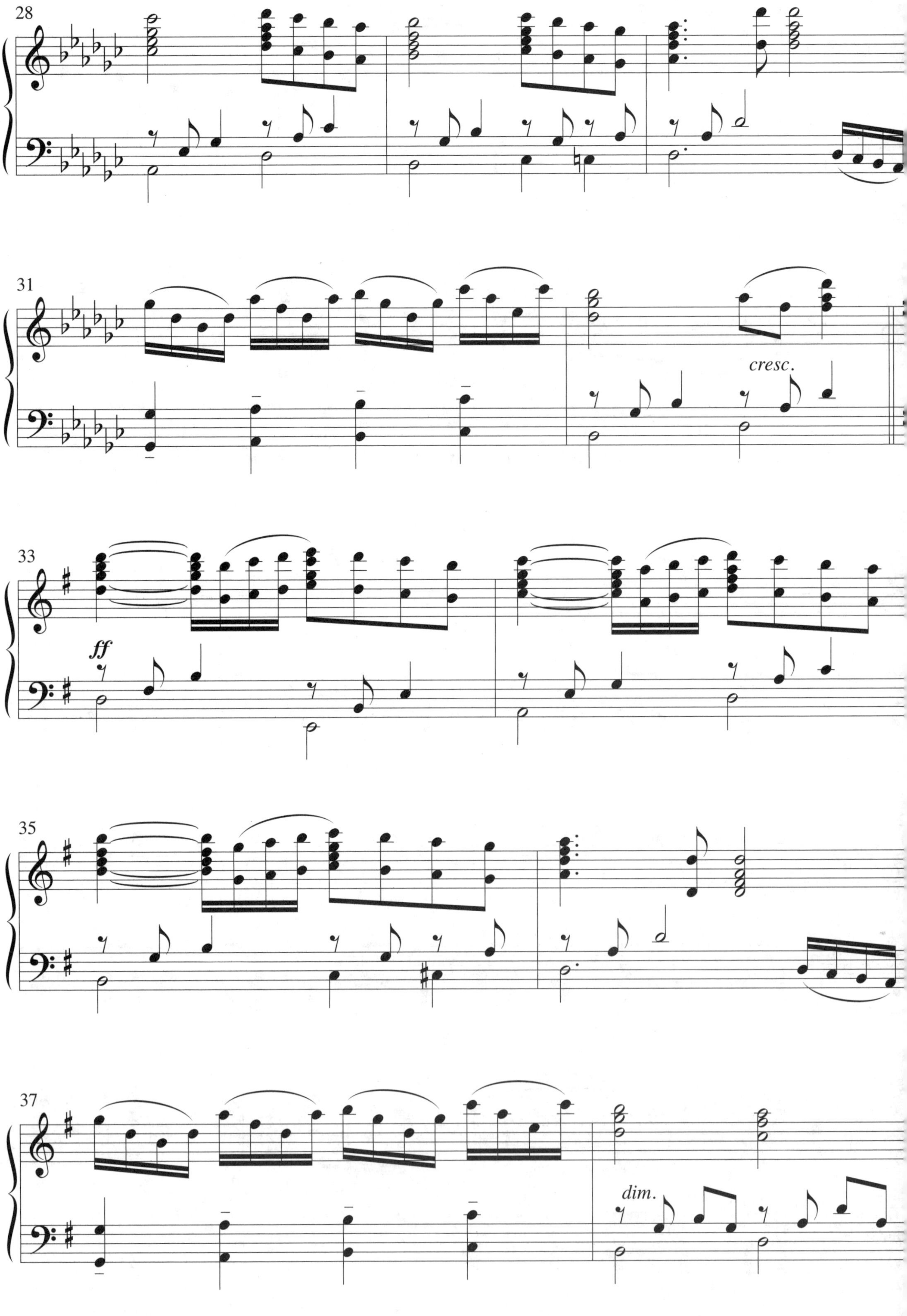
28
31
cresc.
33
ff
35
37
dim.

*"Angels, from the Realms of Glory"

Music by HENRY T. SMART.

*"Hark! the Herald Angels Sing"

*Music by FELIX MENDELSSOHN.

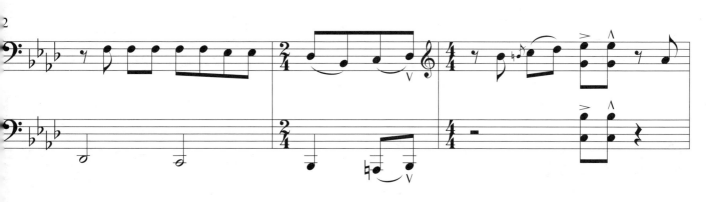

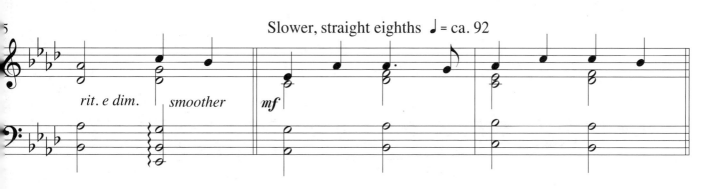

Thou Didst Leave Thy Throne

with
What Child Is This?

TIMOTHY R. MATTHEW
Arr. by Alex-Zso

*"What Child Is This?"

Faster ♩ = ca. 126

Music Traditional English Melody.

Good Christian Men, Rejoice

with
We've a Story to Tell to the Nations

Traditional German Caro
Arr. by Alex-Zso
*"We've a Story to Tell to the Nations"

*Music by H. ERNEST NICHOL

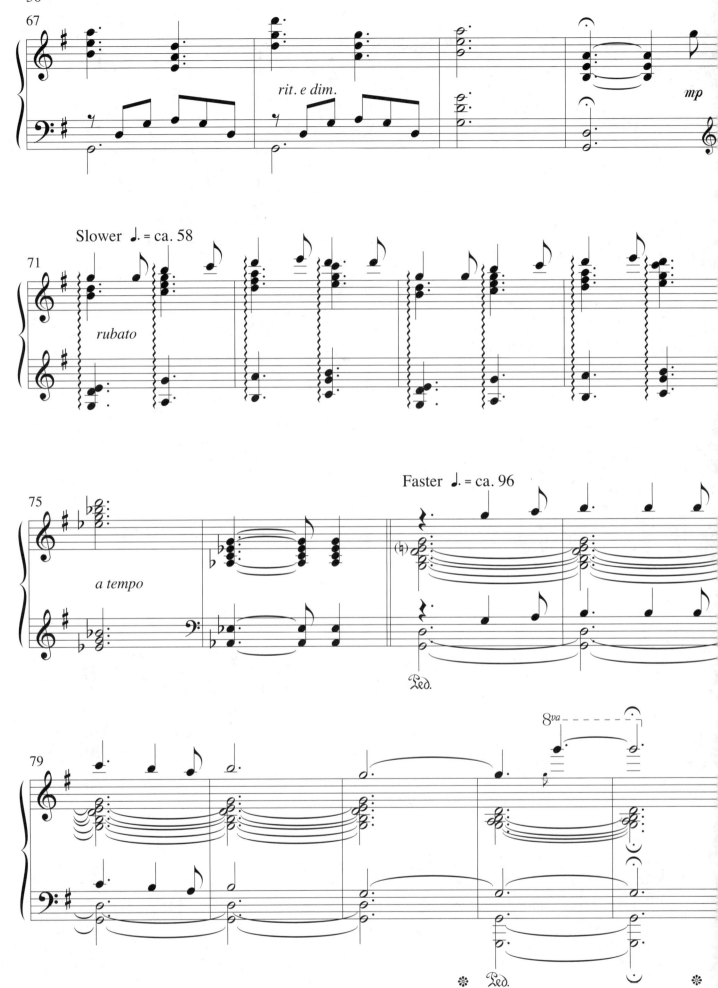

We Three Kings

with

The Birthday of a King

JOHN H. HOPKINS
Arr. by Alex-Zsolt

*"The Birthday of a King"
Worshipfully ♩ = ca. 76

Music by WILLIAM HAROLD NEIDLINGER.

O Little Town of Bethlehem

with

It Came upon the Midnight Clear

LEWIS H. REDNER

Arr. by Alex-Zso

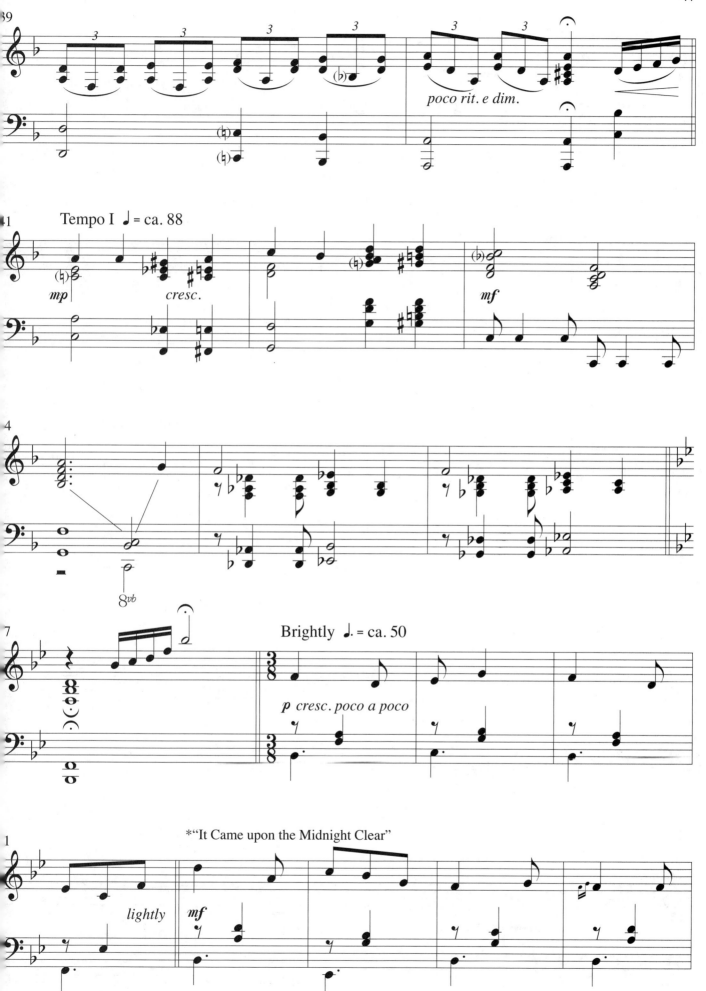

*"It Came upon the Midnight Clear"

Music by RICHARD S. WILLIS.

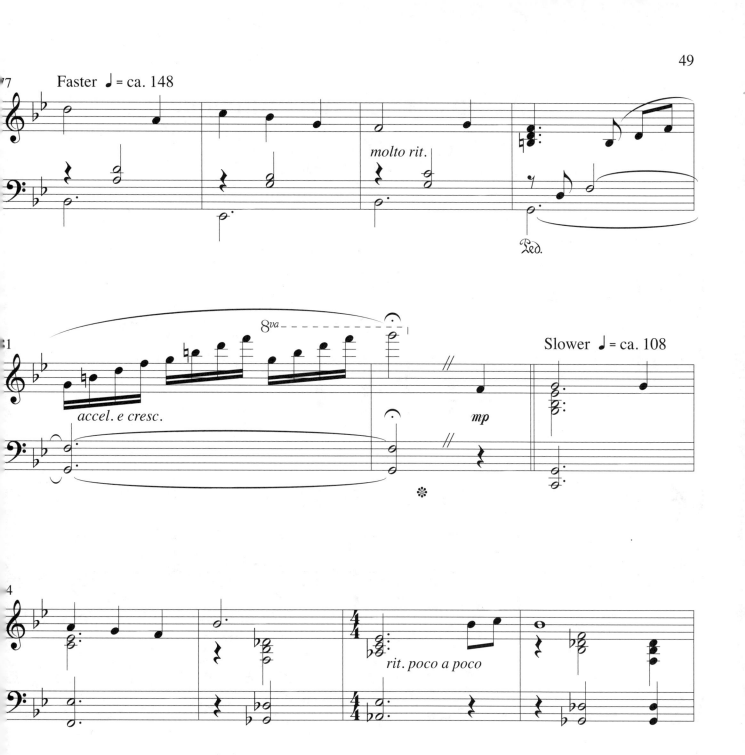

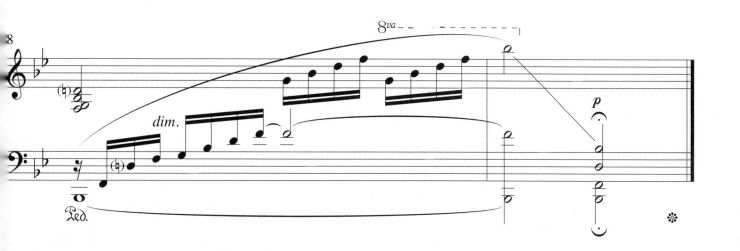

O Come, O Come, Emmanuel

with
Come, Thou Long-expected Jesus
O Come, All Ye Faithful

Plainsong
Arr. by Alex-Zsol

*"Come, Thou Long-expected Jesu[s]

*Music by ROWLAND H. PRICHARD.

Jingle Bells

with

Deck the Halls
O Christmas Tree
We Wish You a Merry Christmas

JAMES PIERPONT
Arr. by Alex-Zsolt

Festive ♩ = ca. 154

Straight eighths ♩ = ca. 154

43

dim. poco a poco

46

p   *rit.*

"Deck the Halls"

49   Slower and reflective ♩ = ca. 90

mp

52

55

mf

Music Welsh Air.

*"O Christmas Tree"

Slower and reflective ♩ = ca. 90

Faster ♩ = ca. 132

Music Traditional.